On the Road to Freedom

On the Road to Freedom

Journey to Becoming Debt Free

Becky McClain

Writer's Showcase
presented by *Writer's Digest*
San Jose New York Lincoln Shanghai

On the Road to Freedom
Journey to Becoming Debt Free

Writer's Showcase
presented by *Writer's Digest*
an imprint of iUniverse.com, Inc.

For information address:
iUniverse.com, Inc.
5220 S 16th, Ste. 200
Lincoln, NE 68512
www.iuniverse.com

Unless otherwise noted, Scripture quotations are from the King James
Version of the Bible.

ISBN: 0-595-14325-3

Printed in the United States of America

I am proud to dedicate this book to my family
—my mother, Willie Mae, my brothers,
Charlie and Clifford and my sisters, Jo and Betty.

EPIGRAPH

Let us lay aside every weight that so easily beset us, and let us run with patience the race that is set before us. Looking unto Jesus the Author and Finisher of our Faith.
(Hebrews 12:1-2)

CONTENTS

LIST OF ILLUSTRATIONS

LIST OF TABLES

Appendices:

FOREWORD

ON THE ROAD TO FREEDOM is a much-needed guide to deliverance for the many Christians who are struggling with financial bondage. I have found this book, written by my dearest friend, Becky McClain, to be insightful and pragmatic. Becky gives personal testimonies and sound financial advice in addressing the issues of God-ordained financial freedom. She writes with clarity and undergirds each chapter with scriptural references. This book will be a blessing to any who read it and to all who apply it.

Maxine Hunt, D. Min.

PREFACE

There are no debt statistics available to specifically assess the condition of the Church. Yet, given the Christian sector in proportion to the overall population, I believe it would be safe to conclude that debt is an issue in many Christian households. In all likelihood, you know someone right now who's struggling with debt.

Debt can directly restrict where you can live, shop, vacation and sometimes work. It has the power to confine one from many conveniences that others simply take for granted. To be excluded from a life that one desires can be quite unsettling. Especially when the exclusion is of ones own doing. The struggle with debt is the external result of an internal virus. It can surface in the form of the "flesh" diseases of poor self- discipline, sacrifice and control—"I have to have it *now*".

The good news is that there is an antidote. If you're struggling with the repercussions of your unwise financial choices, I wrote this book for you. Having stood where you're now standing, I'm going to share how I came through and what I learned during the process. This is a book of compassion, motivation and encouragement. It's also a book of instructions and personal application. At the end of each chapter you'll be given the opportunity to journalize your answers to specific questions. These exercises are designed to provoke you into taking an honest assessment of your past choices. Their ultimate purpose is to enlighten you to a pattern of behavior that you'll need to alter when making decisions in the future. The results will be invaluable.

I believe there is another level of blessings being bestowed upon the people of God. I don't want get left out. To be caught in this wave, we must be spiritually prepared to handle the outpouring. It's the internal transformation that paves the way for external manifestations. The process of debt elimination deals with the root of the problem. It might sound a bit disturbing to refer to a certain problem as a disease. Yet the truth of the matter is, the underlying cause of debt is a spiritual malady—a disorder. I didn't want to face it at the time but as I later assessed my situation, I had to be honest with myself. Of course, there can be unforeseeable crises that arise and leave us overextended, such as medical bills. According to statistics, however, the primary reason most people become strained is due to credit card debt.

I often meditate on Jeremiah 29:11. God knows the plans He has for us financially—great and mighty plans. He has plans that will make an eternal difference in the lives of many people. I believe God is calling us to boldly step out in faith and trust Him with our financial resources. His ultimate purpose might be larger than you; nevertheless, He won't forget you in the process.

I pray that the Holy Spirit will apply to your heart the instructions and principles contained within this book. I believe your faith will be greatly rewarded having taken one giant step toward financial freedom. Open your mind and heart and allow the Spirit of God to teach you.

ACKNOWLEDGEMENTS

Special thanks to:

Bishop James Morton for granting me permission to incorporate titles from his sermon series, *On the Road to Freedom*, into this book.

Rev. Kerwin Lee and Dr. Maxine Hunt for their insight in critiquing the manuscript.

Heithey Williams for patiently proofreading the manuscript several times.

My sister, Betty Morris, for her encouragement throughout this project and all I've endeavored to do. I love you, Sis.

Very special thanks to Patricia Mines and Renita Mathis for contributing their literary expertise to this project.

INTRODUCTION

First of all, let me explain what this book is not. It is not about building wealth and becoming a millionaire. Neither is it a book listing the best stock picks for your investments. Although it is based on Christian principles, there is no mention of the phrase "miracle debt cancellation", which might fly in the face of everything you've been taught about debt elimination.

ON THE ROAD TO FREEDOM was written as a practical application manual to steer you through the first phase of your journey toward financial freedom, becoming debt free. As implied, there is more than one phase to becoming financially free, but that's another book.

This book will also serve as a red light to alert those who have managed to steer clear of the enemy's snare. By exposing the dark side of debt, you'll avoid those pitfalls. Why suffer through an ordeal when you can learn a valuable lesson from someone else's trial?

The Evolution of Debt

How and why did consumer debt evolve? The origin of consumer credit goes as far back as man can remember. It started with a person or business having a product or service to sell. The price was either too far beyond the reach of the average person or the payment for the product was not convenient at the time of sale, thus the beginning of consumer credit.

For example, an automobile is priced at $20,000. The manufacturer must sell many vehicles at this price in order to make a profit. But how many people can put down $20,000 in one lump sum? If the manufacturer only sold automobiles to people who could afford to pay in one lump sum, he would sell very few cars. Consequently, the price would skyrocket from $20,000 to $200,000, due to the manufacturer's need to make a reasonable profit. On the other hand, the manufacturer couldn't make any money if he sold the same automobile for $800. Therefore, the manufacturer must make it available to people who don't have the entire $20,000.

Another example can be traced back to the General Store days, when the payment for products or services was inconvenient at the time of sale. A merchant (or creditor) typically offered payment terms, usually within 30 days. The patron would pick up a few things, charge them to an open account and agree to pay the entire account by the end of the month.

Those days are practically long gone, replaced by major credit cards and department store cards. But the principle is still the same. The difference, however, is that today, you never have to completely pay off a charge account. As long as you pay the interest on the account or the minimum payment, you can continue to charge to the account, up to the credit limit, without ever paying off the original debt. Unfortunately, this is how a lot of people have gotten into serious trouble by amassing more debt than they can afford to service.

Although the credit concept was never intended as a snare to the consumer, the enemy has used it to trap millions. One of his primary mediums has been through advertising. From promoting vacations to vehicles, the media has played a significant role in the state of our financial affairs with its temptations to splurge. Advertising within itself is a wonderful marketing concept. It only becomes a problem when consumers exceed their means of acquiring these goods and services.

Whether it's power, sex, money or material possessions, the devil's subtle enticement is still the same, *"Why put off for tomorrow what you can have today?"*

The Challenge of Debt

We're going to journey through the process of ridding unsecured debt. Unsecured debt includes credit cards, student loans, medical bills, personal loans and any other non-collateral loan. I'm not including secured loans such as automobile and home loans, and I'll explain the reason later in the book.

So that you don't get the cart before the horse, I'll guide you through the process of becoming debt free. I do want to emphasize that it is a process. For too long we, as Christians, have been seeking an instantaneous resolution to our financial dilemmas. We have a tendency to pray and ask God to miraculously cancel our debt through technological and spiritual intervention. However, just as your debt occurred over a course of time, so will your deliverance.

There are those who avoid endeavors that are costly, or things that require self-denial, self-restraint, and self-sacrifice. Freedom comes with a price. Throughout history, major reforms always followed sacrifices. I'm reminded of the lives that were sacrificed during the Civil Rights Movement in which African-Americans and other minorities gained many freedoms.

Make no mistake, I believe in supernatural intervention, but if God were to miraculously cancel all our debts, He'd only be placing salve on the sore. The process of ridding ourselves of debt teaches us the principles of sacrifice, discipline and self-control. God is not in the business of bestowing miracles just for the sake of miracles. We can only reap rewards when we can learn and grow from the process. My journey has taught me one thing…I can say with conviction, *"I'll never go down that road again"*. You'll never appreciate the purpose until you've been through the process.

Financial pressure can affect every area of your life. The primary cause of divorce is money—debt, mismanagement or lack thereof. I'm sure you are aware that financial bondage affects the state of our churches and the means of propagating the gospel of Jesus Christ around the world; it can even affect one's self worth.

The Solution to Debt

In the first chapter, I share my own journey. God provided what I needed when I needed it. If an unexpected financial need arose, He provided. He'll do the same for you. He won't require you to take a journey and then leave you to your own devices. He'll walk with you every step of the way.

During your journey, I'll travel with you through each juncture. We'll take a detailed look at your options so that you can decide on the best course of action for your circumstances. I'll also reveal how to avoid falling prey to the pitfalls along the way and help you devise a personal budget to help track your finances. In addition, we'll review the Biblical purposes for money, which will help to prevent future debt recurrences.

By sharing my journey and eventual destination, I pray that you will be both encouraged and motivated to make the decision that, you too, will walk in perfect liberty. Enough said, let's get started.

FACTS AND FIGURES

❖ Consumer debt stands at $1.26 trillion. More than $540 billion is in revolving credit (credit card loans), compared to $425 billion in auto loans. The remaining consumer debt includes boats, trailers, student loans, mobile homes and vacations.

❖ The average household has four credit cards, with balances around $5,000 (up from two credit cards and $2,340 in balances six years ago).

❖ On average the American consumer will spend 115% more on a credit card purchase than a cash purchase.

❖ Look at your credit card statements: 40% to 90% of the money you pay each month is applied to finance charges. The average credit card will take fourteen years to pay off. You might end up paying back five times the original amount charged.

❖ Consumer bankruptcy filings are at record levels. Consumer bankruptcy filings for 1996 = 1.1 million, 1997=1.33 million and 1998 = 1.34 million (estimated). That is one bankruptcy for every 75 U.S. households.

❖ Millions of consumers are members of a Debt Consolidation Organization.

❖ More than 60% of the credit reports have negative information. Millions of consumers have never seen their credit report.

❖ Approximately 21% of home loan applications are turned down.

❖ Only 3% of the homes in America are paid for.

❖ Nearly half of all American consumers have less than $10,000 saved for their retirement.

Chapter 1

Let the Journey Begin

You will never win if you never begin.

–Robert H. Schuller

There I sat, March 21, 1990, embarrassed and afraid. My financial woes had finally taken their toll on me. As the consumer credit counselor confirmed the state of my financial affairs, I fought back the tears and wondered how I'd ever gotten into this predicament.

It all gradually began during my college years. Getting a credit card was as simple as signing your name on the bottom line. Young and naive, I never considered the consequences of saying, *"Charge, please."* High interest rates, late fees and penalties were all disguised behind the lure of *"Buy now, pay later."* I wasn't aware of the correlation between my payment history and my credit report. In fact, I'm not even sure I was aware that such a file existed. Somehow, with a part-time job and the grace of God I was able to manage one credit card.

The debt began to subtlety amass when I secured my first full-time job after graduating from college. First VISA, then Optima (with cash advances) and the biggie, the American Express gold card. Of course, I'd use self-control by purchasing only what I needed, I reasoned. As you might guess, the necessities included everything from furniture to linen, gifts, clothes...got to have clothes!

As the debt mounted I could only afford the minimum payments each month. There was no noticeable change in my balance from one month to the next. It was like sawing away at a one hundred-year-old oak tree with a nail file. All my efforts seemed futile. Then came the phone calls—you know the ones, before Caller I.D! Before I knew it, I was performing a juggling act, borrowing from Peter to pay Paul. Cash advances from Optima to pay VISA, a part-time job...and on and on it went.

I needed help. I was thirty-three years old, making a salary that was more than enough to meet my needs, if only I were living within my means. What could I do? Where could I turn? Drained and burdened, I finally told the Lord that I wanted to be free.

One day as I was watching television, I noticed a commercial by the Consumer Credit Counseling Service (CCCS). It had probably run many times in the past, but on this particular day I took notice. After listening, I wanted to know more. I wondered if the organization could help me. An inquiry by telephone peaked my curiosity even more. I requested and received information and after reading it, I knew in my heart that this was the breakthrough I needed.

For a couple of weeks I wavered. I went from faith to fear to faith again. Then I went for broke. I cut up all of my credit cards and scheduled an appointment. On a cold, rainy winter day, I began a journey that I'll never regret for the rest of my life.

Waiting in the lobby at CCCS seemed like an eternity, but eventually I heard my name called. A very pleasant gentleman introduced himself as my counselor. On the desk before him were my application, credit history and debt schedule, which I had prepared and mailed in earlier. He assured me that my case was certainly not the worst he'd ever seen and that his agency could provide the help that I desperately needed.

He first assessed my list of monthly expenses relative to my income. He began to eliminate some unnecessary expenses and cut back on others. I was open to his guidance, however, I stood firm when he questioned my commitment to tithing. Regardless of how desperate I felt, I knew I had to put God first. I thank God he didn't press the issue. After evaluating my financial profile, I was told that a three-year debt management program would be required in order for me to become debt free.

Throughout the session my disposition was about as downcast as the weather outside. The negative thoughts came, *"What if...what if...?"* As hard as I tried, I couldn't suppress the tears any longer. My counselor paused briefly and handed me a tissue. I'm sure he had become accustomed to varying degrees of emotions. As I dried the tears, he reached into a desk drawer and handed me a photocopied print. It was a three-dimensional print that I didn't immediately recognize. He instructed me to first look up into the ceiling light and then re-focus onto the print. Feeling absolutely foolish, I acquiesced. To my surprise and amazement I saw the silhouette of a traditional image of Jesus. Moreover, I felt the presence of God giving me the overwhelming assurance that He was with me.

By the end of the session, I felt a sense of peace and confidence. My counselor extended a comforting embrace and assured me that everything would be all right, and off I went.

I wish I could tell you that it was smooth sailing from that point. The truth is, there were times I wanted to throw in the towel. The years that followed required a great deal of sacrifice and perseverance. There were temptations to overcome and pitfalls to avoid.

About a year and a half into the program, my three-year journey turned into a five-year marathon. It was 1992, at the height of corporate downsizing when my employer decided to relocate to New Jersey. Without much deliberation, I knew that relocating to New Jersey wouldn't be a wise move. I was given nine months to prepare for the phase out.

With a small severance package in hand and an airtight job market, I decided to start my own consulting business. Within a few short months I had depleted my severance pay. Sadly, I had not established a solid client base with which to support myself. Nevertheless, I persevered. Unfortunately, CCCS didn't include my automobile loan in the debt repayment plan and before I knew it, I was delinquent. I was juggling between the car payment and CCCS payment. My payments became too inconsistent. CCCS released me from the program.

Another Crossroads.

No longer a part of CCCS, I had to deal with my creditors directly. This time I was wiser. I contacted them all, explained my situation and set up payment arrangements that I could afford. Two years passed; my income steadily increased and the struggle lessened. I was eventually able to eliminate the debt. I had to re-establish a good credit rating. It took longer than I originally anticipated but I endured until the end. Today I'm debt free.

Since then I've secured a mortgage loan, which is a collateral loan. I receive numerous pre-approved credit card and loan offers, but I have no desire to return to the bondage of debt. I've been on both sides of the fence, and believe me, this side is definitely greener.

I hope you're encouraged by my journey to freedom from debt. If I can do it so can you. For some of you, it may take only a month or two. For others, like myself, the scenic route might be the best course to take. Perhaps you won't have to change courses in mid stream. I don't why God led me down a path that wasn't straight and narrow. However, I do know that it served a purpose, if for no other reason than to help someone later.

Because I've traveled this road, I'll ride along with you and help keep you focused on your destination. I'll help make the bumps easier to absorb and veer you back on course should you waver toward defecting. Not only will I be your coach but your cheer-leader as well.

Yes, I'm trying to get you "psyched up" for the journey, because I know what awaits you at the end. God has a plan for your finances, but you can't set that plan in motion if you don't get on board. I'm excited, how about you?

I will instruct thee and teach thee in the way which thou shalt go:
I will guide thee with mine eye. (Psalm 32:8)

* * *

Chapter One Journal

Were you surprised by the debt statistics? To how many can you presently relate?(%)

What impact, if any, did my story have upon your resolve to become debt free?

CHAPTER 2

THE KEYS TO FREEDOM

The path of least resistance and least trouble is a mental rut already made. It requires troublesome work to undertake the alternation of old beliefs. Self-conceit often regards it as a sign of weakness to admit that a belief to which we have once committed ourselves is wrong. We get so identified with an idea that it is literally a "pet" notion and we rise to its defense and stop our eyes and ears to anything different.

–John Dewey

The very first step toward financial freedom is to acknowledge the fact that you need to be free. We often have a false sense of freedom because we measure it by the wrong standard. You're not free simply because you know others whose financial profile is worst than yours. Don't think of yourself as a master juggler simply because you've been able to maintain good credit ratings. You must *cancel* your debt if you want to be absolutely free.

In the book of Daniel, we read the story of how Daniel was taken captive from his homeland in Judah by the King of Babylon. Daniel and his three Hebrews friends, Shadrach, Meshach and Abednego were committed to God and refused to eat meat from the king's table or worship any other god beside Jehovah.

Although Daniel was assigned to the position of a servant, his gift of dream interpretation brought him before kings. The Lord gave Daniel favor with the highest-ranking officials in Babylon. He was even appointed by King Darius to govern over the entire Medo-Persian empire. Daniel was blessed. Nevertheless, as blessed and influential as Daniel was, sadly enough, he was still in captivity. Look at the book of Daniel 9:3 –Daniel fasted, prayed, wore sackcloth and ashes; He says, *"So I earnestly pleaded with the Lord God to end our captivity and send us back to our own land "*. (Living Bible) Daniel didn't have a false sense of freedom—he would much rather to have been back in his homeland than live in the king's palace. Don't think for one moment that his three Hebrew friends were content with Babylonian slave names. They longed to be identified by their free names: Hananiah, meaning "the Lord shows grace"; Mishael, meaning "who is like God?"; Azariah, meaning "the Lord helps".

Perhaps you would have settled into a life of contentment. After all, you're eating good, living in decent quarters, have a little authority and rubbing shoulders with prominent people. Wake up! You don't *own* the palace, you're just a squatter and contrary to popular opinion, squatters don't have any rights. God doesn't want his people blessed in captivity. He wants His people blessed in perfect liberty.

How to Know You're Not Free

Most people will readily acknowledge that they're in financial captivity. For those of you who might have trouble facing that reality, I've taken the liberty of helping you put matters into perspective. How do you know you're not free? You know you're not free when:

1. You're living from paycheck to paycheck
Some people have become so accustomed to barely making ends meet that they've just accepted it as a way of life. What's worst is the common practice of dipping into the next paycheck. There's a better way.

2. Inability to pay off credit card balances at the end of the month
This is the granddaddy of them all. It's the primary reason most people are in bondage to debt and the primary reason I've devoted this book to consumer debt. The rate of revolving credit (credit card loans) is more than 1.25 times that of automobile loans.

3. You don't have at least three (preferably six) months of living expenses set aside
It's very important that you plan for emergencies. Unforeseen circumstances arise—job, health, family, home and auto-related emergencies often arise. The blow is softened having a cushion to fall back on. Single people should be particularly mindful of this point. For example, a job loss to a single person can be especially difficult because there's no spouse to help cover the exposure.

4. You're not a tither
No matter how bad your financial situation may be, you can't afford to close this window. If you don't put God first in your finances, you've got His hands of blessings tied. He can't freely bless you as He desires when you're deliberately disobeying His Word. When you tithe, you're creating a channel through which blessings can flow.

It's no wonder so many in the church suffer lack in their finances. I was surprised to learn that, in most churches, only 20% to 25% of the membership are tithers. It's rather perplexing to witness the magnitude of Believers who show up in droves to hear the Word, yet the enemy steals the seed and prevents it from taking root in their hearts.

Tithing is not a gimmick and if you expect the blessings of God in your finances, you can't bypass this command.

5. You have poor spending habits

You must employ wisdom if you're going to be a good steward. If you have trouble exercising control over your money, you're in bondage. Shopping whenever you have "extra" money will keep you bound. We often justify this 'mindless spending' in God's name. There have been countless times when I've heard people say, *"I'm walking by faith and trusting God to supply my needs as they arise."* Rubbish!

6. You're borrowing from Peter to pay Paul

This is a true telltale sign of someone heading toward financial disaster. You can perform a juggling act for only so long. You are now at the stage where you need to bring your finances into order.

Juggling is mentally draining when you're trying to keep all of your creditors at bay. Rather than paying VISA this month you pay Master Card in order to keep them from calling. Next month, you only pay half of your telephone bill and apply the remainder to your American Express card, in an effort to prevent it from becoming thirty days past due—it's a vicious cycle.

7. The creditors are calling

This is a debtor's worst nightmare. It's like being a fugitive on the run. The harassment and threats can be intimidating. Some creditors will garnish your wages. This is usually the stage at which most people are forced to seek help. It is also at this stage where many people file for bankruptcy protection. That's not one of the alternatives we will consider on our journey because statistics show that the majority of consumers are not on the verge of bankruptcy. However, if you happen to be one of the increasing number who are considering bankruptcy protection, I would suggest that you first seek counsel from a financial advisor.

8. Your Debt Increases as Your Income Increases

If you can't seem to reach that threshold where "enough is enough", you have an insatiable appetite that needs to be satisfied. Unfortunately, some people must go beyond their limit before making a change. You've heard the stories of people who earned millions of dollars only to lose it all in a relatively short period of time. They're never satisfied. The more they earn, the more they spend. You might wonder how anyone could possibly earn $10 million and end up broke. It's easy —poor financial decisions, including debt.

9. You're Working More Than One Job

The Bible says in Psalm 127: 2, "*It is senseless for you to work so hard from early morning until late at night, fearing you will starve to death; for God wants his loved ones to get their proper rest*". (Living Bible) Some people have become burned out from trying to dig themselves out from being underneath a mountain of debt. It is difficult to remain both personally and professionally effective if you're consistently pushing your body and mind to their limits. You won't be able to enjoy the lifestyle you're working so hard to sustain.

10. You're Behind on Your Mortgage

The thought of foreclosure will deter the average person from including their mortgage payment into their debt-juggling act. Although you're not likely to be foreclosed upon for being a month or two behind, you are walking a tight rope here. Unlike revolving credit or utility bills, partial mortgage payments will not temporarily avert the lender.

I'll stop here. I think you get the picture. I didn't list these categories to discourage you but to awaken you to the fact that you might not be as free as you think.

If any of these categories describe your financial picture, you're not alone.

Making the Decision to Become Debt Free

The second step toward becoming debt free is to make a decision that you're going to do what it takes to become free. This was the point at which I struggled with the *"what ifs"*:

What if an emergency arises and I don't have cash?

What if I need to reserve a car, hotel or airline ticket?

What if I want to take a vacation?

What if it takes a long time?

The enemy will barrage your mind with a legion of *"what ifs"*. I'd like to suggest two things to help ward off the *"what ifs"*. The first is the Word of God. Find Scriptures that address financial wisdom, debt, perseverance, faith and freedom (you might come up with others tailored to your specific *"what ifs"*). Jot them down on slips of paper and place them where you'll see them each day (bathroom mirror, refrigerator, car, etc.). Here are a few that I came up with:

Now the just shall live by faith. (Hebrews 10:38)

Owe no man anything, but to love one another; for he that loveth another hath fulfilled the law. (Romans 13:8)

The Lord shall open unto thee his good treasure, the heaven to give the rain unto thy land in his season, and to bless all the work of thine hand: and thou shalt lend unto many nations, and thou shalt not borrow. (Deuteronomy 28:12)

Commit thy way unto the Lord; trust also in him; and he shall bring it to pass. (Psalm 37:5)

Jesus said unto him, If thou canst believe, all things are possible to him that believeth. (Mark 9:23)

The rich ruleth over the poor, and the borrower is servant to the lender. (Proverbs 22:7)

For which of you, intending to build a tower, sitteth not down first, and counteth the cost, whether he have sufficient to finish it? (Luke 14:28)

I have neither lent on usury, nor men have lent to me on usury. (Jeremiah 15:10)

Be not thou one of them that strike hands, or of them that are sureties for debts. (Proverbs 22:26)

And we know that all things work together for the good of those who love the Lord and are the called according to His purpose. (Romans 8:28)

Mediate on these Scriptures and speak them aloud. The Holy Spirit will help you to overcome the *"what ifs"*.

Visualize Your Freedom

Another cure for the *"what ifs"* is to visualize the blessings that await you at the end of your journey. Once again, make a list of what being debt free will mean to you personally. Here are a few to consider:

- Peace of mind

- Give more

- Go back to school

- Purchase a home

- Start a business

- Invest for the future

You alone know the priorities in your life. Your list of blessings will be tailored to your specific lifestyle and aspirations.

You might think that posting and quoting Scriptures and writing down future blessings are a bit extreme. Drastic times call for drastic measures.

This chapter could arguably be the most important chapter in the book. It is the gateway through which you *must* pass in order to reach your destination. By facing the truth of where you are and overcoming the obstacles that will seek to derail you even before you leave the station, you've laid a solid foundation upon which the subsequent chapters will be built.

Congratulations! You're now on your way to a successful journey.

Fear not little flock; for it is your Father's good
Pleasure to give you the kingdom. (Luke 12:32)

* * *

Chapter Two Journal

Of the ten "in perspective" categories, write down the ones for which you can presently relate? (%)

What obstacles will you need to overcome in order to make the decision to become debt free?

CHAPTER 3

CHOOSING THE RIGHT COURSE

If one does not know to which port one is sailing, no wind is favorable.

—Seneca

You're now at the station, ticket in hand, ready to board the train to freedom, but wait, wait, wait! Before you get on board, you need to do a final check with the conductor to make sure you want to travel this route. Once this vehicle is set in motion, there's no turning back.

If you're familiar with traveling, you know that there are several modes of transportation from which to choose. You can travel by airplane, bus, car, train, boat or even walk. If you choose to travel by plane, there are still other choices you'll have to consider. You can either choose non-stop or catch a connecting flight in another city before resuming to your final destination. You can also choose whether you want to ride in first class, business or coach, smoking or non-smoking, window or aisle. Choices, choices and more choices! People who travel by plane usually want the luxury of getting to their destination by the most expeditious means possible. The other modes of transportation are for the more leisurely –they're not in a rush to reach their destination.

Some people enjoy viewing the mountains and countryside along the way.

The decision as to which mode of transportation to take depends upon various factors, not the least of which is money. Along with the "creature comforts" come expense. Another factor to be considered is time. Many people value their time immensely, thereby selecting the quickest and shortest route possible. All things being considered, the choice is left up to the individual traveler.

As it is in the world of transportation, so it is on your journey to becoming debt free. You're going to have to make a choice about the method best for you. After careful research, I selected the following three choices:

◆   Debt Consolidation Organization

◆   Home Equity Refinancing

◆   Personal Budget Plan

I prayerfully chose these three methods because I want to address those of you whose financial profile has not reached extreme proportions (bankruptcy, judgements, etc.), yet you recognize and acknowledge that you need to be free.

Debt Consolidation Organization

If your credit card debt has become burdensome, you're receiving telephone calls from creditors or barely making the minimum payments each month, I would strongly suggest a debt consolidation organization such as Consumer Credit Counseling Service. Although there are other debt consolidation organizations, I recommend CCCS because of my first-hand experience, its long history of service and proven track record.

CCCS is a nonprofit organization that provides free credit counseling and offers debt repayment plans for consumers who are over extended. CCCS negotiates with creditors to reduce or eliminate interest charges for clients who repay their credit through Debt Repayment Plans.

How the Program Works

Rather than reporting negative information to your credit file, many creditors will usually post a note in your file stating that you are under credit counseling. Once you've completed the plan CCCS will help to re-establish your credit.

The enrollment time will depend upon how much debt you owe and the amount you can reasonably afford to pay each month. There is a monthly, tax deductible administrative fee of $5 to $15 that can be waived in some instances.

CCCS is primarily funded through contributions from creditors participating in the program. Creditors generally discontinue the harassing phone calls after receiving three prompt and consecutive payments. Peace of mind at last!

For other debt management organizations, you can use your Internet browser and search keywords "debt consolidation". As a precautionary measure, I would recommend checking with the Better Business Bureau before soliciting any unfamiliar businesses.

Home Equity Refinancing

Home Equity Lending is borrowing additional money against your homestead—borrowing more than the existing loan on the property. As with any loan there are closing costs to be paid that can be rolled back into the loan. Illustration I is an example of a typical home equity loan.

You'll have to apply wisdom with this option or you could end up creating more debt. Consider the remaining balance and term left on your existing mortgage, as well as current mortgage rates before making your decision. By applying a financial or amortization calculation, you can create a schedule forecasting your new mortgage, which you can use in comparison to your existing mortgage. How long have you lived in this house? Do you plan to live in this house for the duration of the term? Would it make sense to refinance when you only have a few short years remaining on your existing mortgage? What will be the term of your new loan? What are the estimated closing costs on the new loan? Answer these questions and weigh yours options. A little logic and a financial calculator will help you decide whether or not it's a good time to refinance.

Computer users can forecast values with what-if analysis in an accounting spreadsheet:

Example:
PMT(rate,nper,pv)

> Rate is the interest rate for the loan.
>
> Nper is the total number of payments for the loan.
>
> Pv   is the present value, or the total amount that a series of future payments is worth now; also known as the principal.

The following formula returns the monthly payment on a $25,000 loan at an annual rate of 9 percent that you must pay off in 24 months:
=PMT (9%/12, 24, 25000) equals -1142.12

Example:

A two-variable data table can show how different interest rates and loan terms will affect the mortgage payment. In the following example, cell C2 contains the payment formula, =PMT(B3/12,B4,-B5), which uses two input cells, B3 and B4.

List of values substituted
in the row input cell, B4

	A	B	C	D	E
1	**Mortgage Loan Analysis**				
2	Down Payment	None	$ 384.46	180	360
3	Interest Rate	8.50%	8.00%	$477.83	$366.88
4	Term (months)	360	8.25%	$485.07	$375.63
5	Loan Amount	$50,000	8.50%	$492.37	$384.46

List of values substituted in
the column input cell, B3

The primary advantage of the home equity loan is to consolidate your debt into one monthly payment with a *lower interest rate*, thereby creating a *lower monthly payment*. Another advantage of consolidating high-interest rate credit card balances is that mortgage interest is tax deductible.

Before deciding on this choice, be sure to carefully read the lenders loan restrictions and guidelines which contain many safeguards for both borrower and lender. Close scrutiny of these guidelines will also help to determine if a home equity loan is right for you.

Sample—Home Equity Refinancing

Current Mortgage Balance	$75,000
Closing Costs	$2,175
Equity Borrowed	**$10,000**
Gross New Loan Amount	$87,175
Term of Loan	30 years
Appraised Value	$115,416
Interest rate on new loan	7.5%
Principal and Interest	$609.52
Taxes	$175.00
Insurance	$38.00
Total Payment	$822.52
Closing Costs on New Loan	
Loan origination fee	$865.00
Appraisal fee	$325.00
Credit report	$60.00
Loan processing fee	$100.00
Title insurance settlement fee	$100.00

Title insurance	$605.34
Recording fees	$40.00
Title company courier	$45.00
Tax certificate	$35.00
Total Closing Costs	**$2,175.34**

Illustration I

This option might appear to be contradictory to your overall objective. But, I included it because statistics reveal that only 3% of the population own their homes. Unless you can afford to purchase a home with a lump sum, you will probably service a mortgage loan. Why not use the equity in your home to consolidate your debt?

Personal Budget Plan

It is possible to eliminate your debt without any profession assistance or refinancing your home. It could simply be a matter of restructuring and prioritizing your financial affairs. In the next chapter, we'll take a snapshot of your financial portfolio and devise a strategy that will guide you through this choice.

A significant portion of the remainder of the book will be concentrating on this alternative. It is the one option for which no second-party assistance is readily available. In fact, this book will serve as the second party.

Subsequent chapters will also assist in maintaining a debt-free lifestyle.

Calculate Your Debt

Now that you're aware of your three options, take the time to total up all of your credit card balances. Student loans, medical bills and any other unsecured debt should also be tallied. I was surprised to learn that many people are intentionally unaware of the cumulative amount of their debt. This is where you'll have to face those fears head on.

Cut Up the Credit Cards

This might just be your boldest act yet. Cut up all of your credit cards and immediately notify your creditors to close these accounts. It's important that you do this now, otherwise you might be tempted to resume charging at a later date.

Making Your Choice

In summary, if you are burdened or over extended by debt, you'll need to seek out professional assistance by contacting your local Consumer Credit Counseling Service or other comparable agency. Schedule an appointment to discuss their Debt Repayment Plan.

You should choose Home Equity Refinancing to consolidate you debt after factoring in current mortgage rates, balance and term remaining on current mortgage versus a new mortgage. This is the most immediate remedy, however, that shouldn't be your only consideration. Your credit history will also be a major factor to be considered in home equity refinancing.

If your debt hasn't become a burden, yet you want to maximize your earnings, the next chapter will provide illustrations to help monitor your spending habits.

Regardless of the course you choose, be sure to prayerfully weigh all options before making your final decision. Make your selection based upon your circumstances and the sacrifices you're willing to make as you make your way to the "Promised Land".

There is a way that seemeth right unto a man, but the end thereof are the ways of death. (Proverbs 14:12)

* * *

Chapter Three Journal

Which method will you utilize to become debt free? Why?

Are there other alternatives you've considered? What are they? Why?

CHAPTER 4

THE ROAD MAP

Your goals are the road maps that guide you and show you what is possible for your life.

–Les Brown

Interstate 285 encircles metropolitan Atlanta. If you decide to merge onto I-285, eventually you will arrive back at your starting point. If you never exited the freeway, you would aimlessly wander around in circles for hours. You must have a destination in mind.

Have you ever been traveling in an unfamiliar city and gotten lost? A road map would have given you the bird's eye view you needed to direct you to your destination.

Trying to attain debt freedom without a budget would be like wandering aimlessly on I-285—absolutely no direction. A budget is the road map you'll need to gauge your progress, track your finances and keep you on target.

In this chapter we're going to review a sample budget and walk through the preparation of your personal budget. Our sample budget illustrates Jane Doe as a single parent with one dependent child. Her annual income is $40,000, which includes a salary and child support. Her total credit card debt is $6,000. Jane's goal is to eliminate the outstanding balances on these accounts.

Take a look at Illustration II at the end of the chapter. This illustration shows Jane's entire payment structure after having her financial profile reviewed by her financial advisor. Highlighted in Illustration II are seven charge accounts that were recently closed, with a payment allocation for each account. Later in the chapter, we will actually walk through the process you'll need to reach this point.

Illustration III gives a breakdown of how the payment allocation for each account will be applied. Column C shows the outstanding balances on the start date of her journey, which is July 1. Column D is the annual interest rate that was taken directly from her monthly statement. The monthly interest rate in Column E was also taken from her statement. It can also be calculated by dividing the annual interest rate by 12—a good checks and balance measure. The payment allocation percentage in Column F was computed by dividing the balance of each account by the sum total of all accounts. The monthly payments in Column G were derived at by multiplying the percentages in Column F by the cumulative amount of the monthly payments in Column G. This cumulative amount ($357) was determined after all *ordinary and necessary* expense payments had been established. You'll need to prepare your personal budget before you can determine this amount.

Illustration IV gives a timeline for eliminating Jane's debt. She can actually project the length of time it will take to cancel her debt by preparing a monthly account activity schedule in advance. By applying a simple formula, Jane knows that she will be debt-free within the next twenty months.

Before moving on to the next section, you'll need to get a clear understanding of the three illustrations to help draft your personal schedules. If necessary, walk through the illustrations again with a calculator.

Reviewing Your Financial Situation

Your Personal Budget worksheet can be found in the Appendices section. Use the worksheet to pencil in your financial information. Computer users might want to set up their own form onto a computer spreadsheet. Formulas can be set up to automatically calculate many of the fields. You will have more flexibility to edit.

The first step is to record your monthly income from all sources including part-time work, child support, alimony, etc. The more sources you are able to include in your debt elimination process, the shorter your timeline.

Next, sum up and record your monthly expenses. On a separate sheet you'll also want to total and record all occasional expenses such as car insurance, oil changes, clothing, garbage pick-up, etc. Don't fail to include entertainment and recreation expenses, which most often reflect the discretionary income consumed. Divide these occasional expenses to derive at a monthly budget expense for each item. Although these expenses are not paid on a monthly basis, you'll need to make an allowance in your monthly budget so that they will already be accounted for when they become due. I would advise you to set aside the money in a special account. Avoid accounts with easy access and you'll avoid unnecessary temptations. When a payment becomes due, you can simply transfer the money into your regular checking account.

Be sure to account for every expense including your credit card payments. There's no need to be concerned about the net effect of your income and expenses. If you find you're actually spending more than your income, we'll deal with that shortly.

Our next step is to assess your financial situation based on this recorded data and develop your personal road map. Place a check mark beside all ordinary and necessary expenses. Ordinary and necessary expenses are those expenses you must incur in order to maintain your livelihood, such as food, utilities, rent, etc. Cable television and housekeeping services are conveniences—not necessary expenses. This is where you may want to cut back or eliminate some of your entertainment and recreation expenses. If your expenses exceed your income, you'll need to look at other areas in which to cut back and/or eliminate for a season. Perhaps you'll need to carefully examine dining expenses, cable services, and hair and nail expenses. You may also want to inquire about utility budget plans.

During my journey and subsequent intervals, I've given up shopping for a season. Styles don't change so rapidly that you can't go without shopping for a year or two. You can mix, match and accessorize to keep your look updated. This is where a change in your thinking comes into play because you might feel the "need" to purchase new clothes. Many people purchase clothes to impress others, but you'd be surprised to know that other people probably won't even notice that you haven't purchased a new outfit in over a year. What if they do? You're on a mission. Take care of what you have and wear it with confidence. I use clothing as an example because of the emphasis placed on clothing and the percentage of discretionary (and unfortunately *non-discretionary*) income consumed in this area.

I also cut back on dining out so frequently. In fact, I went through a season of packing my lunch and carrying it to work every day, which led me to establish better eating habits and a more healthy diet. A healthy diet, in turn, led me to become more conscientious about maintaining a consistent exercise routine. Sacrificing does have its benefits.

Once you've streamlined your monthly expenses, decide on an amount to set aside in a special account for emergencies and those times you simply need to splurge. Although it's important to stay on course, allow yourself to participate in events and activities that were not specifically listed in your budget. However, don't get carried away here. You'll notice in the illustration that Jane set aside $100 a month in a special account for her occasional expenses, emergencies and "mad money." With the amount remaining you're going to apply to eliminating your credit card debt. In our example, Jane is applying $357 per month to her credit card debt.

Let's determine how the $357 will be allocated to each account. A blank Unsecured Debt Payment Allocation form is available in the Appendices section you to work from. Once again, it might be wise to set up your own form onto a computer spreadsheet for flexibility and accuracy. For spreadsheet users, you'll find the same form with the formulas set up in the cells.

Gather all of your credit card statements and fill in your payment allocation form or spreadsheet as shown in Illustration III. In Column C enter the account balance for each credit card at the end of the previous month. In Column D and E, enter the annual and monthly interest rates, respectively. Column F and G can be calculated by following the example in Illustration III. This illustration allocates to each account an amount in proportion to the percentage of each credit card balance to the total debt, as shown in Column G. This is your monthly expense for each account, which you'll need to transfer to your budget.

Illustration IV will actually give you a timeline for completing your journey. By completing this spreadsheet you're able to project the pay-off date by applying the account activity for each month going forward.

On your account statements, depending upon the interest rate and balance, you'll notice that the interest is applied to the average daily balance. Because all your accounts have been closed, you'll apply the interest to the account balance. In computing the interest, you'll need to refer back to Illustration III, Column E. You can adjust your payment amounts as your income increases.

Because this projection might be lengthy, I would strongly advise you to set up Illustration IV onto a computer spreadsheet. Set up formulas in the cells to automatically calculate rather than manually calculating each cell. You'll find a form containing the formulas in the Appendices section.

This sample presupposes that the credit card interest rates are relatively the same. However, if you have higher interest rates on some cards, you might want to adjust your payment allocation percentage to apply a larger amount to the higher interest rates. With my personal budget, I applied the allocations as illustrated, without adjusting for higher interest rate cards. Remember, as your income increases, you'll adjust your payment schedule accordingly. Weighing both the account balances and interest rates, it all balances out in the end.

You now have the road map you'll need to complete your journey. I want to emphasize that this journey should not make you feel like a prisoner. We oftentimes feel locked in when held to a certain amount of structure in our lives. However, structure is precisely the ingredient you'll need in maintaining your freedom once your journey's complete.

SAMPLE

PERSONAL BUDGET

INCOME: July, 1999	1-Jul-99	15-Jul-99	Total
Gross Income	1,417	1,417	2,834
Deductions: Taxes, health insurance	(569)	(479)	(1,048)
Other Income: Child Support	500	0	500
Net Income	**1,348**	**938**	**2,286**
EXPENSES:			
Tithes	335	0	335
Save (includes occasional expenses)	50	50	100
Mortgage	500	0	500
Car Note	0	200	200
Auto Insurance (occasional expense)	0	0	0
Automobile—fuel & cleaning	50	50	100
Oil Change (occasional expense)	0	0	0
First Union Master Card	54	0	54
Chase Manhattan VISA Card	29	0	29
Neiman Marcus	71	0	71
Sears	46	0	46
Wal-Mart	46	0	46
Chevron (gas card)	22	0	22
Haverty's Furniture	89	0	89
Clothes	0	75	75
Lawn Care	25	25	50
Electric (utility)	40	0	40
Gas (utility)	40	0	40
Telephone (utility)	50	0	50
Water (utility)	20	0	20
Garbage	10	0	10
Cellular Phone	0	0	0
Pager	0	0	0
Cable TV	0	0	0
Food	125	125	250
Bank Service Charges	15	0	15
Nails	10	0	10
Hair	0	50	50
Personal (toiletries, etc.)	15	15	30
Entertainment—movies, dining, music	29	25	54
Total Expenses	**1,671**	**615**	**2,286**

Illustration II

SAMPLE

UNSECURED DEBT
PAYMENT ALLOCATION

B	C	D	E	F	G
CREDIT CARD ACCOUNTS	Account Balances @ 6/30/99	Annual Interest Rate	Monthly Interest Rate	Payment Allocation Percent	Monthly Payment Amount
First Union Master Card	$ 900.00	20%	1.67%	15%	$ 53.55
Chase Manhattan VISA	500.00	19%	1.58%	8%	28.56
Neiman Marcus	1,200.00	16%	1.33%	20%	71.40
Sears	800.00	21%	1.75%	13%	46.41
Wal-Mart	750.00	16%	1.33%	13%	46.41
Chevron (gas card)	350.00	19%	1.58%	6%	21.42
Haverty's Furniture	1,500.00	21%	1.75%	25%	89.25
Total	6,000.00			100%	357.00

Illustration III

Calculations:

First Union Master Card
Payment allocation percent
$ 900.00 / 6,000.00=15%

Monthly payment amount
$357.00 x 15% = $53.55

Annual interest rates and allocation percentages rounded to the nearest whole number

Note: Budget figures may vary slightly due to rounding differences

SAMPLE

MONTHLY ACCOUNT ACTIVITY
AND
TIMELINE PROJECTION

B	C	D	E	F
	6/30/99			**7/31/99**
ACCOUNT ACTIVITY	**Balance**	**Interest**	**Payment**	**Balance**
First Union Master Card	$ 900.00	$ 15.00	$ (53.55)	$ 861.45
Chase Manhattan VISA	500.00	7.92	(28.56)	479.36
Neiman Marcus	1,200.00	16.00	(71.40)	1,144.60
Sears	800.00	14.00	(46.41)	767.59
Wal-Mart	750.00	10.00	(46.41)	713.59

Illustration IV

Calculations:

First Union Master Card

Interest (Column D)

$ 900.00 x 1.67% = $15.00

(Account balance x monthly interest rate)

End of month balance (Column F)

($900.00 + $15.00)-$53.55= $861.45

(Account balance + interest-payment allocation)

Note: Figures may vary slightly due to rounding differences

In all thy ways acknowledge him, and
he shall direct thy paths. (Proverbs 3:6)

* * *

Chapter Four Journal

What are your spending weaknesses?

How do you feel about sacrificing for an extended period of time?

CHAPTER 5

JOURNEY PARTNERS

Friends are as companions on a journey, who ought to aid each other to persevere on the road to a happier life.

–Pythagoras

It's easy to get discouraged and turn back when you're traveling an obstacle course all alone. Companionship gives you someone with whom you can share your journey. As I look back, my journey could have been smoother had I a partner to walk with me along the way.

I was too embarrassed to share my plight with anyone. In more recent years, I've learned the true financial state of many in the Body of Christ. A very significant portion of the Church is in bondage to creditors. God wants his people free!

I strongly suggest that you seek out someone with whom to travel on your road to becoming debt-free. Your partnership can provide you both with a spiritual support system. Let's take a look at some partnerships found in the Bible. They will help you in selecting someone to share your journey.

David and Jonathan

David and Jonathan were male soul mates. They were in covenant together. The Bible says in I Samuel 18:1-3 that the soul of Jonathan was knit with the soul of David. Jonathan made a covenant with David because he loved him as his own soul. A word of caution here, though. Although David symbolizes the *Spirit* and Saul, King of Israel, symbolizes the *flesh,* in the final analysis Jonathan's covenant with David did not transcend family ties. Sure, Jonathan helped David but he died following after his father, Saul. He knew right from wrong, but in the end he chose flesh over Spirit.

As a Believer who is walking according to the Spirit of God, you cannot be in covenant with a carnal Christian. Being unequally yoked can result in worldly, fleshly counsel when seeking advice concerning your finances: *"Hide the car, don't answer the phone, pretend you're not home, cuss 'em out."* Ungodly counsel.

We all know people with godly wisdom who'll guide us in the right direction. They won't tell us what we want to hear or sugarcoat the truth. Those are the people who will help us to grow not only in matters concerning our money but also our Christian character. Don't share your situation with someone who will only fuel your temptations.

Mary and Elizabeth

The story of Mary and Elizabeth is one of my favorites. Take a few minutes and read the account of their relationship in the book of Luke, Chapter 1. Elizabeth and Mary had something in common; they were both pregnant. Not only were they both pregnant, but the circumstances surrounding their pregnancies were miraculous. After the angel convinced Mary that she would give birth to the Savior of the world, she danced and sang praises to God. Afterwards reality set in. How would her fiancé, Joseph, receive this "wonderful" news? Can you imagine Joseph's reaction when

Mary told him she was carrying a child conceived by the Holy Spirit? Apparently he didn't believe her because the Bible says that he sought to "put her away" privately in order not to publicly disgrace her. It took God Himself to persuade Joseph not to call off their engagement. If that wasn't enough, let's not forget about Elizabeth, who was seen out-and-about pregnant long past childbearing age. What a sight!

The Bible says that Mary visited Elizabeth and stayed for three months. That's a long visit. I believe they utilized that time to strengthen and encourage each other because their circumstances were difficult. Mary sought out Elizabeth because she was family and also because she could identify with being ostracized. Elizabeth provided Mary with love, protection and emotional support. Mary awakened Elizabeth's motherly instincts. Together they could rejoice because they knew that the rejection they were experiencing would ultimately be to God's highest glory. They knew that God was faithful and that His timing was perfect.

Perhaps you have a family member who is also under the weight of debt. Family members are generally sincere and tend to be very protective. When you are both dealing with the same dilemma, you can provide emotional support one to the other. Family members will usually stick with you until the very end. They're not likely to jump overboard before the journey ends.

Naomi and Ruth

Naomi and Ruth were related by marriage. Naomi was Ruth's mother-in-law. Their bond was formed as a result of family tragedies. Read Chapter 1 of the Book of Ruth to get an understanding of the background of their relationship.

Naomi took Ruth under her wings, so to speak, and converted Ruth from her pagan religion. She provided motherly guidance and, in Chapter 3, she even gave her step-by-step instructions on how to win the heart of Boaz. Ruth was vulnerable in a new land, amongst an unfamiliar people and culture. She trusted Naomi's wisdom and advice and in return she was devoted to Naomi and provided sustenance for their family unit.

Many times older Christians in the church have already gone through what you're dealing with and can provide much needed guidance. By sharing their experience and of how the Lord brought them through, you will be encouraged. Rarely have I been inspired and motivated by someone giving me advice without having experienced what I'm experiencing. *"God will make a way"* just doesn't cut it for me. The Bible says that we overcome by the Blood of the Lamb and the words of our testimony. (Revelation 12:11)

Paul and Silas

Paul and Silas were a rare breed. Anytime you can sing and shout in prison after being beaten and shackled, you're head and shoulders above most. Even though my natural response is to complain, I'm learning to praise God in the midst of my trials.

We don't learn much about Silas in the Scriptures, however, like Paul, Silas was a leader and prophet in the Church of Jesus Christ. In fact, he traveled with Paul on his second missionary journey. On the contrary, we know Paul's history. Paul, formerly known as Saul, persecuted the Church. He hated Christians and led a revolt to destroy them until he was blinded on the Damascus Road. He wasn't aware that he was on his way to his own destruction. It was only by the grace of God that Saul was converted to Christianity. Paul had reason to praise God.

You have to be *in Christ* in order to praise God in the midst of difficulties. A shallow relationship with Jesus won't suffice during turbulent times. However, if you've reached the level where God has first place in your life and is the center of your affection, you can shout in the midst of a storm. When the enemy comes with his suggestions and *what ifs*, call up your praise partner and shout the victory. Deuteronomy 32:30 says that one can put a thousand enemies to flight and two can put ten thousand to flight.

Jesus and His Church

As important as family, friends and other Christians are to your journey, no one can replace your personal walk with Jesus. Jesus has the power to change your circumstances or change you in the midst of your circumstances. He may not supernaturally cancel your debt, but He'll provide what you need to make it through. And always remember that He's teaching you something in the process. Perhaps He's testing your faith or teaching you self-control and discipline. He's a good God and He takes no pleasure in seeing you struggle. I'm a living witness that He'll walk with you every step of the way.

I pray that you won't take this chapter lightly because you might be surprised to learn of the strength you can gain by sharing your situation with someone you can trust.

You might want to establish a time each month, over lunch or dinner, to share your progress and struggles. This would be a perfect time for you both to re-affirm your commitment to the process and rejoice in your victories.

It's always encouraging to know that you're not alone. Remember in I King Chapter 19 how depressed and abandoned Elijah felt when he thought he was the only prophet left who hadn't bowed to Baal. The devil will try to discourage you by making it appear that your sacrificing is in vain, while others around you are being blessed. Don't be fooled by appearances; concentrate on doing what you know is best. A partnership will go a long way in helping you both achieve your goals.

As you go along, you will become accustomed to the change in spending habits and the challenges will gradually give way to excitement. You'll have peace knowing that your life is going to be better. Visualize yourself standing atop that mountain of debt. You'll be able to *taste your freedom*. After all, you are more than a conqueror. (Romans 8:37)

As you move closer to freedom, you might even find that you no longer need human support; you can cast that load onto Jesus and let Him carry it for you. He delights in carrying our loads.

Can two walk together,
except they be agreed? (Amos 3:3)

* * *

CHAPTER FIVE JOURNAL

Who will you select as your journey partner? Why?

What do you have in common with your partner?

Chapter 6

Moving Forward

---

*Learn to adjust yourself to the conditions you have to
endure, but make a point of trying to alter or correct conditions so that they are most favorable to you.*
                                        —William Frederick Book

If you were to travel on a non-stop flight from Atlanta to
Nashville, you probably would not have time to watch a movie.
You'd be arriving at your destination about mid-way through the
movie. It's a short flight; approximately 75 minutes. Typically, on
short flights you're only served light refreshments. However, if
you were to travel on a non-stop flight from Atlanta to San
Francisco, not only would you have ample time to watch a movie,
you'd get a meal to boot—and perhaps a snack. The flight time
can range from four to five hours. Along with the additional
amenities of a longer flight, the traveler can become restless. For
starters, they might decide to read a book. Shortly thereafter, they
might want to take a nap. They shift positions —first toward the
stranger to their right and then back toward the stranger to their
left. "How much longer?" they ask themselves.

Sound familiar? As realistic as the above scenario, you could
become spiritually or emotionally restless on your debt-free
journey. The longer the journey, the greater the opportunity to

become weary. If you chose the home equity refinance option as an alternative to consolidate your debt, the timeline could be compared to a non-stop flight from Atlanta to Nashville. The timeline will be relatively short. But what if you don't have a home or qualify for the refinancing alternative? Should you opt to go with a personal sacrifice or debt repayment plan, your journey could be compared to a non-stop flight from Atlanta to San Francisco. In other words, you could possibly get a little restless along the way.

It's going to take some time for you to adjust to your lifestyle change. What do you do in the meantime? The most important thing you'll need to do is to change your thought processes. There are some factors that you'll need to adopt if you're going to counteract periods of weariness that will seek to deter your forward progress.

The Focus Factor

If you're going to move forward you can't spend your time looking backward. Neither can you straddle the fence. You've heard it before but it bears repeating—you need to detach yourself from people and things that will cloud your focus. You might need to announce to certain people what your goals are so that they don't hinder you from making progress. Perhaps you have become accustom to shopping with your friends every Saturday. If shopping is an area you've chosen to sacrifice for a season, you have an announcement to make. Don't allow the enemy to deceive you into thinking that you can just go along for the ride. Don't try to exercise willpower—just stay out of the mall.

Before I went through the journey process I rarely prepared meals at home. I didn't realize the amount of money I was consuming on a monthly basis dining out. One of the changes I had to make was to reduce the amount of money I spent eating out, which was practically every meal! It took some adjusting but I eventually came up with a plan that I could live with. I'd often carry along a magazine or book to keep myself occupied while eating the salad and sandwich I'd packed for lunch. It was important that I didn't venture out to run any errands during my lunch break, because I'd inevitably be tempted to cheat. Initially, I had to make a conscious effort to stay on course.

There may be other areas that you'll need to put the past to rest. The important thing is to keep your eyes on your goal. I've always been told that whereever I go in life, not to burn any bridges. That might be good advice for the business world, however, on this journey there are some bridges you'll need to burn if you're going to move forward. Philippians 3:13-14 states it thusly: *I count myself not to have apprehended: but this one thing I do, forgetting those things which are behind, and reaching forth unto those things which are before, I press toward the mark for the prize of the high calling of God in Christ Jesus.*

As important as it is not to look back, it's equally essential that you not look too far ahead. You could become discouraged focusing on the length of time it will take to completely pay off your debt. You could also paint an unrealistic picture out in the distance.

It's perfectly all right to calculate your timeline projection. I'd even advise you to prepare your budget six months ahead. Yet, you only want to work with a weekly-to-monthly snapshot. While you don't want to paint a picture of gloom, you don't want to get a false sense of security either. You *will* make a few tweaks in your budget along the way. You can't always account for the unexpected. You want those modifications to have only a minor impact on your budget. To summarize the point, focusing on the short-term will help you keep your priorities in order and avoid overspending.

The Faint Factor

There might be times when you become discouraged and want to give up. You might feel it's too difficult to remain focused or it's taking too long to reach your goal. I know the feeling very well. It's during these times that you'll have to draw upon your spiritual strength.

The story of Abraham and Sarah in Genesis Chapter 15 will help you put your situation into perspective. God promised them a son when Abraham (Abram) was seventy-five years old and Sarah (Sarai) was sixty-five. We'll deal with their ages later, but for now let's focus on the promise. Twenty-five long years passed before they received their son, Isaac. It's no wonder God never revealed to them the length of time before the fulfillment of the promise.

As we pick up the story in Genesis Chapter 16, we learn that Sarah and Abraham didn't wait very well. They concocted a scheme that they would later regret. Rather than waiting on God's timing, they decided to help God out by delivering a son through Hagar, Sarah's handmaiden. They suffered the consequences for this big mistake. Everyone involved in the circle of events surrounding their bad decision was adversely affected. Hagar mocked Sarah because Sarah was barren. Sarah blamed Abraham because their little scheme blew up in their faces. Abraham wouldn't stand up and take any responsibility. Isaac was jeered and insulted by Ishmael, Abraham's son through Hagar. Finally, Hagar and Ishmael were banished from their home. All of this drama occurred because Abraham and Sarah fainted.

Having to sacrifice two or three years is miniscule compared to twenty-five years. We now live in a society that has made *waiting* an obsolete term. Modern technology has created a "push button, at-your-fingertips" civilization. I was recently withdrawing cash from an Automatic Teller Machine that asked if I wanted to purchase stamps or a prepaid telephone card. There are even Internet grocery stores that will deliver to your door. Not only do they deliver groceries, they also deliver flowers, office supplies and drug store items. Go figure!

As alluring as modern technology has become with its innovations, there are some things in life that cannot be achieved without waiting. God masterminded it that way, because waiting builds character. Waiting teaches endurance, strength, patience and self-control—just to name a few. How we wait also determines how long we wait. If you wait in frustration and bitterness, you'll only extend the semester! If you refuse to wait, you'll fail the course and, in turn, have to repeat the class—either now or later.

My relationship with Jesus is solidified during my times of trial. I find myself listening more intently when the Word is being taught. I also spend more time in prayer and meditating on the Word. I expect to hear what the Lord is trying to convey. He has exposed some of my baggage and allowed me to see my own weaknesses. Oftentimes we're not even aware of the "cancers" growing inside of us until the Lord begins extracting them. It's usually painful and unsettling, because we believe we're okay. As He begins to stretch you, the key is not to faint. He's not trying to hurt you—He only wants to root out those little imperfections and character flaws. He'll comfort you as you humble yourself before Him. As you draw near to Him, He'll draw near to you. (James 4:8)

The Bible says in Galatians 6:9, *Let us not be weary in well doing: for in due season we shall reap, if we faint not.*

The Faith Factor

During your journey, your faith will also be tested. Perhaps you've amassed a very large sum of debt and you feel your situation is hopeless. Or perhaps you feel that your case is much different from other people. This is exactly how Abraham and Sarah felt.

When God first approached Abraham and promised him a son the Bible says in Genesis 15:6, *Abram believed God: then God considered him righteous on account of his faith.* Abraham was hopeful and excited. Twenty-four years later God reappears and tells Abraham that Sarah will deliver his promised son in about a year. How did Abraham respond this time? Genesis 17:17 says, *Abraham fell upon his face, and laughed, and said in his heart, shall a child be born unto him that is an hundred years old? And shall Sarah, that is ninety years old, bear?* And how did Sarah respond to this wonderful news? Genesis 18:12 explains, *Sarah laughed within herself, saying, after I am waxed old shall I have pleasure, my lord being old also?* Sarah didn't even believe she could still have a sexual thrill, much less have a baby! They both laughed in disbelief. What happened between Chapter 15 and Chapter 18? Frankly, Abraham and Sarah had a faith failure.

After enrolling in Consumer Credit Counseling Service, I became excited. No more phone calls, no more pressure; I could breathe a sigh of relief. Then the unexpected happened; two months with a new employer I learn that my job was being phased out. Consumer Credit Counseling Service dropped me from their program. I had a momentary faith failure. I became very perturbed and grew a pity party. My question to God was, *"Why, Lord? Only a year and a half left in the program. Why?"*

Within a couple of days my frustration gave way to determination. I refused to be denied. What I discovered was a God-given strength that was revived within me. God was stretching my faith and I was holding on for dear life. I've had many trials in my life, but I can't begin to share the spiritual impartation of this single test.

Regardless of how you might feel to the contrary, you're not traveling a road that has never been treaded. At some point in your Christian walk, your faith is going to be tested, even to the point of disbelief. What I love about the story of Abraham and Sarah is, although they fainted, they still received the promise. They laughed but they still received the promise. In the end, their wavering faith became stable.

It's not as important how you start; what's important is how you finish. *Am I sure that God who began the good work within you will keep right on helping you grow in his grace until his task within you is finally finished on that day when Jesus Christ returns.* (Philippians 1:6, Living Bible) It's perfectly normal to experience momentary lapses in your faith. We live in a natural world where we operate on a sensual level—see, hear, taste, touch and smell. However, we can't rationalize the events of our lives on the natural plane. Our faith transcends into the spiritual realm.

I encourage you to be strong and stand steadfast when the enemy comes and whispers, *"what if"*. It's only a distraction to get you to faint. Don't give in to hopelessness. Don't try to invent your own scheme. God is faithful. Trust Him even to your breaking point. You just might find that you're more equipped than you think.

> *And Jesus said unto him, No man, having put*
> *his hand to the plough, and looking back, is*

fit for the Kingdom of God. (Luke 9:62)

* * *

Chapter Six Journal

What is the greatest obstacle(s) that might seek to prevent you from moving forward?

How do you propose to overcome this obstacle(s)?

CHAPTER 7

THE REST STOPS

Every now and then go away, have a little relaxation, for when
you come back to your work your judgment will be surer.
—Leonardo Da Vinci

Like millions of individuals around the globe, good health is not
something I take for granted. As the years pass, I'm becoming
increasingly aware of the importance that a healthy diet and fitness play in my overall physical well being. I subscribe to a series
of books that address the health needs of women. Some foods I
have restricted from my diet completely, while others I've
decreased my intake. I've also implemented an exercise regimen
that fits my schedule.

I make every effort to include foods and activities that will
reduce my risk of heart disease and other sicknesses. When grocery shopping, I'm careful to read the labels for fat, sodium and
cholesterol content. I know the importance of acquiring my
daily requirements of water, fruits and vegetables, protein and
grain. I must admit that trying to stick to a healthy regimen is a
conscious effort. I enjoy fries, pizza and chocolate cake!
However, I'm keenly aware that regular consumption of these
foods is not in my best interest. And to be perfectly honest, I
don't always feel like exercising. Yet cardio-vascular and

strength training are necessary for maintaining a healthy heart, physical endurance and muscle tone.

As much as I know of the significance of health and fitness, there are those times when I deviate from the program. Although I don't totally throw caution to the wind, there are times when a salad just won't suffice. I load up the baked potato, pour on the gravy and have the chocolate cake too! Occasionally I *need* to deviate from the norm —without any guilt. Come tomorrow, it's back to the shredded wheat, salad and the treadmill. But today, I need a break!

Take a Break

There will be times when you'll need to deviate from your normal routine and splurge. In Chapter 4, I addressed the need to set aside funds in a special account for those times you'll simply need to indulge in your passion. You might want to go on a weekend get away or perhaps patronize one of the finest restaurants in your city. Whatever your passion may be. Might I remind you to only tap into the resources you've set aside for this purpose? Don't spend your rent money! When I mentioned that I needed to take a break from my normal health and fitness routine, I *did* weight in the morning before. Although I deviated, there were certain parameters I had to stay within.

If you've ever driven long distances, you've probably visited rest stops to go to the restroom or just stretch your legs. Many long-distance truck drivers pull off the interstate into a rest stop to take a nap. These minor interruptions in ones routines serve a definite purpose. You'll need to take periodic breaks during your journey in order to endure the course.

Breathe a Sign of Relief

With each successful milestone comes a sigh of relief. You might look back at the previous quarter and be amazed that you were able to stick to your budget. You can splurge without a guilty conscious because you met your goal. Routine breaks will serve as a reward for reaching another milestone.

In the last chapter, I challenged you not to look back at your past. If your past is a reminder of something you long for, then don't look back. However, if your past encourages you to continue moving forward, then it's okay to look back to see how far you've come. Metaphorically speaking, look back and see how you steered around that pothole in the road. How about the way you careened through those glaring lights obscuring your view? You deserve a break. Take time out to celebrate the little victories along the way. But I repeat, don't spend your rent money!

Renew your Strength

If you don't take frequent stops along the way, you're going to grow tired and weary. You've heard of people falling asleep behind the wheel while traveling, because they refused to pull over to rest. You might feel that the less stops on your journey the quicker you'll reach your destination. If you're not alert, you might not reach your destination.

Suppose you have $300 set aside at the end of a quarter to simply splurge. Rather than taking a break, you decide to apply the money to your credit card accounts. Six months are far too long a stretch to restrict yourself from indulging in your passion. Unless you're absolutely sure you can go six months or more on a strict budget, I'd advise you to take a break. I can recall a conversation I had with a young lady who informed me that her company's policy stipulated that accrued vacation time could only be redeemed after the employee's first year anniversary. As you can image, the number of reported sick days was astronomical. If you don't deviate regularly, you could find yourself bingeing with your tithing allowance. Then you're off course, because that wasn't in the plan.

Okay, let's say you've had your little rest stop. It's now time to gear up for the next interval. Taking a break should also get you mentally prepared to move out again. You know you have a long road ahead; therefore, you map out when and where you're going to take your next break. These periodic interruptions are also designed to renew your strength.

When you exercise with weights, you're instructed to take a short break between repetitions. You're also taught not to exercise the same muscles two consecutive days. You need to allow your muscles to rest between intervals. This prevents over exertion and allows you to see the results of your workout. Your strength is renewed for the next set.

Whether the weights are natural or spiritual, the principle is the same. While operating within the guidelines of a financial regimen, you shouldn't feel like a prisoner. Don't lock yourself into a daily grind. You want to be free to exercise some choices as you go. Take some time to indulge in the activities you really enjoy. Breathe a sigh of relief and renew your strength before moving forward again.

And the king, and all the people that were with
him, came weary, and refreshed themselves there.
(2Samuel 16:14)

* * *

Chapter Seven Journal

What level of passion do you exercise in completing a task?

Is your work/recreation ratio out of balance to either extreme? Explain.

CHAPTER 8

BEWARE OF THE PITFALLS

You can have it all. You just can't have it all at one time.
—Oprah Winfrey

There will be temptations and obstacles that will attempt to impede your progress. I'll call them the Four C's. These are hindrances you'll need to overcome, not only during this journey, but also beyond. We'll look at all four in detail: **Comparing** ◆ **Competing** ◆ **Complaining** ◆ **Compromising**.

Comparing

One obstacle you'll need to overcome is the temptation to compare your situation with that of someone else. Don't allow yourself to give in to despair simply because another person's debt-free option released them before yours. The Lord knows what road is best for you. May I remind you again, He not only wants to free you, but He also has something to teach you in the process. One person may be allowed to use the Home Equity Refinancing option and become immediately free, while another may need the assistance of a debt repayment program. Yet another may have the will power to make the personal sacrifices necessary to become debt free without professional assistance.

God knows that an instantaneous solution is not for everyone. If I didn't follow God's path, I would not have the self-control that I have today. Getting back into debt is unappealing to me. I don't want to experience the struggles of the process again. The credit card and loan offers I now receive are immediately discarded without any reservations whatsoever.

It is possible to become debt free in a short period and remain free without having gone through a long process. You could become so frustrated and burdened by all the harassing telephone calls and letters that the stress alone would prevent you from returning. God knows what works for whom. His ultimate goal is that He might be able to trust you and produce the gifts and qualities that you've probably been praying for. Surprise, surprise!

Competing

Another obstacle you'll need to overcome is the temptation to compete with others. Don't allow yourself to be concerned with the blessings of others. Don't become anxious by trying to manipulate people and circumstances in an attempt to compete with others. God saves His best for those who will wait for Him. Your season is around the corner.

This is one of the primary reasons many people experience financial downfalls. They want what they want and they want it now! There's a constant attempt to *keep up with the Jones'*. What they don't realize is that life in the Jones' house just might not be as rosy as it appears.

Competition is actually a worldly principle. There is a healthy competition that motivates others to move to a higher level and helps to bring out their best, which is common among athletes. However, self-destructive competition leads to jealousy, envy and resentment. Resist this temptation and wait on God. You'll be glad you did.

Complaining

God hates whining and complaining. The book of Numbers 11:1 tells how God became angry when the Israelites complained about their hardship. The Bible says that the fire of the Lord destroyed those at the far end of the camp. This Scripture alone emphasizes the passion God feels with regard to complaining. The reason the Israelites wandered in the wilderness for forty years is not because it was God's will, but because of their own rebellious nature. Don't prolong your journey by murmuring and complaining about your struggles. Keep a good attitude. If you'll be honest, I'm sure you'll admit that the Holy Spirit didn't lead you into your financial wilderness.

We often suffer consequences as a result of our complaints and rebellion. God is faithful and loving and when He chastises us, it is out of His love for us. I've been guilty of murmuring because I didn't want to suffer the effects of my poor financial decisions. I'm learning to take my difficulties before the Lord and thank Him for helping me to go through whatever I have to go through—praising Him as I go.

Jesus is our prime example. He never complained to God about anything. I know those disciples got on His nerves, especially Peter! Not to mention the multitude of people he encountered and the Jewish leaders. Nowhere in the Scriptures do we hear Jesus saying anything to the affect, "Father, what have you gotten me into? These stiff-neck folks are about to drive me crazy!"

Compromising

Resist the temptation to take matters into your own hands by attempting to manipulate your circumstances and formulating a short cut.

Not long ago I was in the process of building a new house and only had a few short weeks to make the full down payment. Embarrassed as I am to admit it, I actually went before the Lord and suggested that He allow me to apply my tithes to the down payment on the house. I reasoned with Him that it would only be for a couple of payments, after which I'd resume tithing as usual. As misguided as my thinking was, the sky didn't fall on my head, lightning didn't strike me down and God didn't afflict me with a crippling disease or beat me over the head with a hammer. I was coasting right along. However, now I think I know what Asaph was experiencing when he said he almost slipped until He went into the sanctuary in Psalm 73:17. For me, it was during a revival one night when the Spirit of God convicted me so badly that I immediately repented. I didn't know how God was going to work it out, but I knew I had made a detour and was traveling down the wrong road (even if you don't share it all with your journey partner, you can't outwit the Holy Ghost)! When I repented of my disobedience, God worked it. The house wasn't ready by the completion date and the builder had to extend the contract another thirty days. The Lord bought me some more time.

Don't allow the devil to tempt you to the point of going against God's word. If you'll do it His way, He'll work it out for your good.

There hath no temptation taken you but such is common to man: but God is faithful, who will not suffer you to be tempted above that ye are able; but will with the temptation also make a way to escape, that ye may be able to bear it. (1 Corinthians 10:13)

* * *

Chapter Eight Journal

Why are you in debt?

What would you do differently if you could do it over again?

CHAPTER 9

THE REWARDS OF FREEDOM

Conquering any difficulty always gives one a secret joy, for it means pushing back a boundary line and adding to one's liberty.
–Henri Frederic Amiel

Have you ever witnessed someone suffering and, from the depths of your heart, you wanted to provide for them, but you couldn't? Or perhaps you've wanted to give to other worthy causes, but you simply didn't have the money. These are common occurrences for Christians who are bound by the spirit of debt. Lack of money can have a halting effect on the best of intentions.

Jesus is the Master Financier. He spent an inordinate amount of time on the subject of money because He knew the significance mankind would place on its value. He addressed tithing, sowing, investing, serving, treasuring and hoarding money.

The Bible is clear on the need and purpose for money. In order for us to reap the rewards of financial freedom, it is imperative that we understand the Biblical purpose for it. God's purpose for money is threefold:

To propagate the Gospel–*And he said unto them, Go ye into all the world, and preach the gospel to every creature.* (Mark 16:15)

To help those in need–*But whoso hath this world's good, and seeth his brother have need, and shutteth up his bowels of compassion from him, how dwelleth the love of God in him?* (I John 3:17)

To live an abundant life –*The thief cometh not, but for to steal, and to kill, and to destroy: I am come that they might have life, and that they might have it more abundantly.* (John 10:10)

Propagating the Gospel

Jesus came into the world to seek and save the lost. In the last three years of His earthly ministry He went about preaching the message of salvation and setting the captives free. Jesus gives His mission statement in Luke 4:18-19:

"The spirit of the Lord is upon me, because he hath anointed me to preach the gospel to the poor; He hath sent me to heal the broken hearted, to preach deliverance to the captives, and recovering of sight to the blind, to set at liberty them that are bruised, to preach the acceptable year of the Lord."

As Jesus ascended to His Father, He passed the torch on to His disciples, admonishing them to be His witnesses in Jerusalem, and in all Judaea, and in Samaria, and unto the uttermost part of the earth. (Acts 1:8) How could a gospel that began with only twelve disciples revolutionize the entire world? Through evangelism.

The ministry of evangelism is costly. No longer can itinerant preachers and missionaries who traveled primarily by sea and land evangelize regions around the world. Modern technology such as radio frequencies and television satellites make it instantly possible to transmit the gospel to all nations.

It doesn't cost us to witness to people in our homes, on our jobs and in our communities. However, that's only the tip of the iceberg. God wants to reach the uttermost crevices of the earth. In order to provide the platform for disseminating the gospel around the world, financial resources are needed and those resources must come from the Body of Christ.

It requires billions of dollars to produce television programming and transmit radio waves. In addition, there are Bibles, tapes, tracks, books, etc. produced and distributed for the purpose of winning souls to Christ and edifying His Body.

It is such a gratifying experience to have someone accept Jesus Christ as his or her personal Savior as a result of your personal witness. How much more rewarding than to witness how God is reaching millions of people around the globe as you sow into good-seed ministries that are committed to evangelism at home and abroad.

Living an Abundant Life

This is an area where many people need to change their thinking. Contrary to what you may have heard or been taught, God does not object to Christians being wealthy or living in abundance. In fact, it is not His will for His children to suffer lack and live in poverty. His only concern is that we don't allow money to rule us. The Bible doesn't say that money is the root of all evil, but that the *love* of money is the root of all evil.

A lack of money can strip your joy. One of the most disheartening experiences in life is to have financial obligations and lack the means of fulfilling those needs. Lack has a crippling effect—it can place undue pressure on you. It can even prevent you from sleeping at night.

God knows how much money with which He can entrust us. If we're not faithful with a small amount, He knows that He can't trust us with abundance. He is ready and willing to pour abundance into our lives, but we can tie His hands with disobedience and poor stewardship. In order for God to greatly bless us financially, we must be a giver of what He gives us. We can't expect God to pour into our lives if we refuse to tithe and give offerings for the work of the Church and sow into the lives of others.

Second Chronicles 16:9 says, *For the eyes of the Lord run to and fro throughout the whole earth, to shew himself strong in the behalf of them whose heart is perfect toward him.* He's just sitting ready to bless us, however, it's up to us to get into position to receive. He wants to do exceedingly, abundantly above all that we ask or think, according to the power that works in us. (Ephesians 3:20) I don't know about you, but I can think big!

Helping Those in Need

There are people God wants to reach who have been neglected and given up upon as social outcasts. Jesus was often criticized because he was frequently seen in the company of sinners and those socially unaccepted. He was moved with compassion when he encountered hurting people. The Bible says that He went about healing the sick and doing good.

Our communities are filled with people we need to reach out to with our financial resources. The displaced and at-risk populations in our communities are often overlooked. Not necessarily because people are not concerned but, in many instances, because they are often uninformed or they can't relate to another person's dilemma. I'm sure you've seen people who have become the spokespersons for particular causes after a certain malady hits close to home—a loved one dies or is stricken with a terminal disease. Because they've experienced a personal connection with another party, the illness now becomes a cause that pulls on *their* heartstring.

I attended a presentation given by an organization that provides shelter for homeless women and children. They were making a fundraising appeal for their facility. The homeless women, some pregnant and some with children, were discovered sleeping under bridges, in abandoned buildings and on the streets. This particular organization serves as a sanctuary for those homeless, hungry and hurting women and their children. In addition to food, clothing and shelter, the center provides counseling, jobs, money management and spiritual enrichment.

I must admit that I was somewhat ignorant and slightly removed from the plight of these women, but after having been made aware, I certainly felt compassion for them. So much so, that I became a financial support partner to assist in their development and empowerment, as well as integrating them back into mainstream society.

We can't merely place the burden of responsibility on our churches and government to provide financial support to meet the needs of the at-risk in our communities. Quite often, the funding is simply not available. We're called as individuals to do our part. There are men, women, youths and elderly who are homeless, battered, abandoned and troubled who need our support.

Seek out an organization (or start your own) whose cause is dear to your heart and become a financial supporter. Even if you don't know a charity you're interested in supporting on an ongoing basis, the point is, you shouldn't stand on the sideline. Get involved in helping those in need.

I was recently listening to a local talk show on the radio. The host of the show was a personal finance expert. A gentleman called in with an investment question. He was thirty-two years old. He had invested the maximum amount into his company's 401K retirement plan. His earnings were too high to qualify for a Roth IRA. He had a mutual fund, stocks and bonds. He inquired about other investment options. The host asked him if he had considered giving some of his money away. There was dead silence on the caller's end of the telephone line. I was quite amused by the response to the gentleman's response(or lack of response), because he was so proud of himself. It was obvious he wasn't expecting the answer that he received. Invariably though, she went on to give the caller some tips on real estate. But I was reminded of the story about Jesus and the rich young ruler. The Bible says he came to Jesus inquiring what he could do to inherit eternal life. In the end, he went away sad because Jesus asked him to sell his possessions and give them to the poor. (Matthew 18:16-22) Jesus was only testing him to determine what he treasured most in life. *And the King shall answer and say unto them, Verily I say unto you, Inasmuch as ye have done it unto one of the least of these my brethren, ye have done it unto me.* (Matthew 25:40)

The Rewards of Financial Freedom

Financial freedom produces rewards –not the least of which is peace of mind. Peace is a very liberating force. Even though you might not be wealthy after completing your journey, the pressures of debt will no longer haunt you. You'll have gained control over poor spending habits because you will have learned to live within your means and understand the purpose of money.

The primary rewards that financial freedom offers are more *choices* and *opportunities*—perks in short supply during your stint in the debt wilderness. Instead of the shackles of shuffling and juggling your funds, you're better able to weigh out investment and retirement options. Although financial freedom is by no means the key to happiness, you will enjoy a sense of fulfillment in this area. Just think of the money you've wasted simply for the "convenience" of having debt. Financial freedom allows you to maximize your money. It affords you the luxury of moderately indulging in many diversions that might be enjoyable for your particular lifestyle.

As nice as these many choices are, for me, the greatest reward of financial freedom is to be released from the shackles in my mind and spirit.

And ye shall know the truth, and the truth shall make you free. (John 8:32)

* * *

Chapter Nine Journal

Using the space below, journalize what being debt-free will mean to you.

CHAPTER 10

NOW THAT YOU'RE FREE

The problems that we face today cannot be solved at the same level of thinking we were at when we created them.

—Albert Einstein

In Luke 11:24-26 Jesus teaches a parable about a man who was delivered from a satanic stronghold. Unfortunately, that wasn't the end of the story. This same man later became possessed by seven times more demons. Why? He left a void unfilled. The point that Jesus is making is that once He delivers you, you must take the proper measures to remain free. Your story doesn't have to have a tragic end.

You have to work to hold onto what God has done in your life. Don't let the enemy lure you back into captivity. Let's take a look at how you can fill in the gaps and preserve your freedom.

Make responsible decisions

Don't allow yourself to be pressured into impulsive decisions. Beware of appeals that entice you to *"act now, this offer won't last forever"*. I recently contacted an investment broker to seek advice about some security options. The sales pitch on the telephone was far too aggressive. I deliberately left my checkbook home before meeting with the person. I made a decision beforehand that I wasn't going to allow myself to be pressured into making a commitment that I might later regret.

We encounter numerous types of offers that appeal to our senses. We get so excited by the demonstrations and testimonies that we make hasty decisions. Don't even enter into long-term contractual obligations such as home alarm systems, cellular telephones, etc. without asking three questions: (1) *"Do I really need it?"*, (2) *"Will I use it?"* and (3) *"Can I afford it?"* Some people have gotten locked into long-term health club memberships that they rarely used. Ouch!

Ecclesiastes 2:26 says, *For God giveth to a man that is good in his sight wisdom, and knowledge, and joy: but to the sinner he giveth travail, to gather and to heap up, that he may give to him that is good before God.* He wants to entrust the Body of Christ with large sums of money to establish his covenant in the earth in these last days. However, He's not going to transfer wealth into the hands of a bunch of immature Christians who have no self-discipline. How can God give true wealth if we're unfaithful stewards with what He's already bestowed?

Change your habits

Many Christians operate under the premise that they can be frivolous spenders and look to God later to bail them out. It's true that God often bails out "baby" Christians who are not mature in their walk. But there will come a time when they'll need to advance to a level of accountability. James 2:17 says: *Even so faith, if it hath not works, is dead, being alone.* There must be some action behind your faith.

Began operating on a cash-only basis. If you can't pay cash for that outfit, you don't need it. After a while, it will simply become a way of life. You'll begin gaining control over those impulses and urges.

Plan ahead for major events. If you 'd like to take a vacation in June, don't wait until the last minute before deciding to take the trip. Start setting aside the money six months ahead of time. You'll enjoy yourself and won't be strapped for cash when you return. After returning from your vacation, you should begin thinking about the Christmas season. You won't have to over-spend if you plan ahead.

If you must have a credit card, get one simply for the convenience. Pay off the balance at the end of each month.

Change your thinking

Please don't embrace the world's remedies as your solution to becoming financially free. I hope you're not relying on the lottery as the answer, or that an unexpected check is going to arrive in the mail, or that a computer glitch is going to reverse that bad credit report. These are all signs of spiritual immaturity. Don't sweep your mistake under a rug, hoping that it will magically disappear because it won't. Face up to the fact that you made some unwise financial decisions that resulted in your exposure to debt. A quick fix doesn't get to the root of the problem. You have to change your thinking.

Be led by the Holy Spirit

Don't make financial decisions without consulting the greatest Financier. Ask the Holy Spirit to be Lord of your finances. He will guide you. He will prevent you from entering into those impulsive contractual obligations. He will also led you to bargains and to honest people who won't take advantage of you.

I can certainly look back at some financial doors that the Lord closed in my face. I didn't understand at the time, but I was later able to look back and see His omniscient hand.

The next generation

Teach your children about debt and its consequences. Share your past experiences, including the struggles. Most credit card companies target college students because of their irresponsible spending habits. They realize that the burden will likely fall on the parents. Prepare your children for the onslaught of credit card offers with the "fine print" trap.

Before your adolescent heads off for college it would be a good idea to print out statistical data on consumer debt. The first orientation many kids get at the "University of Finances" is after they leave home. They need to be home schooled on the finer points of spending responsibly.

The future is coming

A few months ago I was on the Internet and stumbled upon an article entitled, "Rich Boy, Poor Man." The article featured former television child stars who amassed a fortune in their youth but ended up squandering their riches. As a result of extravagant lifestyles and poor money management, as adults, they were left with very little and were forced into non-entertainment careers in order to survive.

Paul Peterson, a child star on the "Donna Reed Show" admitted that he thought his future would be secure without making any long-term preparations. What really stuck with me most was his statement, *"It's so easy to forget that the future is going to come."*

Have you stopped to think about how you're going to live after you retire? Surely you don't plan to work forever. Unless you've settled into a simply meager lifestyle, you can't expect Social Security to maintain an above-average standard of living. Some economic experts claim that we shouldn't even rely on Social Security at all. If Social Security is hardly adequate now, I wouldn't take the risk of securing my future solely upon it. Also, have you considered leaving an inheritance to your children or grandchildren? The Bible says that a good man influences four generations.

God is not against us securing for our future. However, He doesn't want us to hoard money to the exclusion of His Church and people in need. In Biblical times wealth was passed down from generation to generation. Abraham was very wealthy and he tithed from all of his possessions. He also passed an inheritance down to his son Isaac.

Put God first

God has a plan for your life, including your money. The area of finance is often the last we surrender to God. Jesus, in His foreknowledge, was keenly aware that there would be issues surrounding money. While in the temple, He pointed out to His disciples a poor widow who had only two mites, yet she put it all into the treasury. The Bible says that she gave out of her need while the others gave from their abundance. She put the Kingdom first.

God rarely asks us to give all we have. When he does test us, His motive is to sift our priorities. If we respond by putting Him first, we never have to worry about our needs going unmet. He never promised that all of His followers would be rich, but He does desire that we all be prosperous. You know you're prosperous when you're walking in liberty physically, economically, emotionally and spiritually.

Stand fast therefore in the liberty wherewith Christ hath made us free, and be not entangled again with the yoke of bondage. (Galatians 5:1)

* * *

Chapter Ten Journal

What lesson(s) has God taught you during your journey?

How will you share your experience?

CHAPTER 11

THE ROAD LESS TRAVELED

I was part of that strange race of people aptly described as spending their lives doing things they detest, to make money they don't want, to buy things they don't need, to impress people they dislike.

–Emile Henry Gauvreau

The secular world embraces the notion that you should get as much of the earth's possessions as you can, as often as you can and however you can. This concept is in stark contrast to God's economy for obtaining blessings. The Bible tells us in Luke 7:38, *Give, and it shall be given unto you; good measure, pressed down, and shaken together, and running over, shall men give into your bosom.* The Bible also stresses the importance of waiting upon God's timing. Psalm 37:34 puts it this way, *Don't be impatient for the Lord to act! Keep traveling steadily along his pathway and in due season he will honor you with every blessing.* (Living Bible)

The world doesn't understand Christians. They don't understand that our joy is not predicated upon our circumstances and surroundings. Nor do they comprehend how we can forgive without trying to even the score. The world believes in luck and positive thinking. Christians believe in blessings and the power of God. The two are diametrically opposed one to another.

I've been praying for an old, unsaved friend for many years now. He called a month ago and asked if I was a tither. My first notion was that perhaps he'd become a Christian. Unfortunately, that wasn't the case. He had heard about the term from another Christian. My response to his question amazed him. He went on to reel off a laundry list of things that I could be doing with "that money." My heart went out to him, because he just didn't understand.

As Christians, we live *in* the world but we're not *of* the world. We're call to travel the straight and narrow rather than the broad and wide road. We don't always understand why the world "seemingly" possesses so much and Christians possess so little. As a result, we often play by their rules and suffer the consequences. Earthly goods are only as wood, hay and stubble in the overall scheme of things. They have no eternal value. *What shall it profit a man, if he shall gain the whole world, and lose his own soul?* (Luke 8:36)

The most important treasure that I gained during my journey was a change in my thinking. I was liberated from my own misconceptions surrounding money. I found out first-hand that the Word of God is a sure foundation. I have nothing to prove, nor do I have a desire to impress anyone. I don't need to covet another man's possessions; God has made promises to me. Many of those promises I'm enjoying today, while others I'm awaiting in quiet anticipation.

Perhaps there are promises God has made you. Your greatest test is to wait. As the world turns, there will always be seedtime and harvest. (Genesis 8:22) Don't allow the world to lure you into its "get-all-you-can-now" system. Keep traveling down the straight and narrow pathway. The best is yet to come!

And be not conformed to this world:
but be ye transformed by the renewing of your mind,
that ye may prove what is that good, and
acceptable, and perfect will of God. (Romans 12:2)

✳ ✳ ✳

Chapter Eleven Journal

Where do you go from here? Explain.

EPILOGUE

With self-discipline, most anything is possible.
                                        –Theodore Roosevelt

Thank you for allowing me to travel with you these past eleven miles. I'm excited about your new beginning because I know that God has a financial plan for your life. My sole purpose for writing this book is because I believe the Lord wants me to use my journey through the debt process to help someone else overcome. He wants His people free.

Although I've never given a widely publicized testimony of God's faithfulness during my times of trial, there were several times in the past that I wanted to share my experience. However, the Prompting within was never strong enough. Now I know that it wasn't the proper time. By no means am I insinuating that I've arrived at some far off, majestic utopia. But I am debt free—at liberty to "exhale."

When the Lord initially impressed upon me to write, I dismissed the idea. After all, I'm not a writer by profession nor has it ever been a desire. However, as I studied His Word and listened intently to His voice, He imparted a desire to use my experience with debt, along with my accounting gifts to combine spiritual principles and practical illustrations to guide the reader through the debt elimination process and beyond.

I'm well aware that there are several books and sermons on the market that focus on debt cancellation, yet I strongly believe God wants to use this simple little book to set someone free. Many Christians dealing with debt can readily identify with my story.

My prayer is that the Holy Spirit will speak to you about your financial affairs and lead you to choose the best course of action. Ask Him to guide you in seeking a journey partner who is best suited to travel with you along the way. I cannot guarantee that there will not be times when you won't be tempted to throw in the towel, because old habits can be hard to break. I will, however, promise that once you've tasted freedom, you'll never want to be bound again.

I've been blessed having written this book. My sincere desire is that God will get the glory and that His purpose might be fulfilled in your life. It's been an honor and a privilege.

His humble servant,

ABOUT THE AUTHOR

As a consultant, Becky advises and prepares financial statements for individuals, small businesses and non-profit organizations. She's been instrumental in the acquisition of a multi-million dollar worship and educational facility. Becky also consults with large corporations to recover overpayment of taxes.

Accounting solutions and tax planning are her specialties. Becky holds a Bachelor's degree in Business Administration from Morris Brown College and an MBA in Accounting/Taxation from Mercer University. She has over twenty years of experience as an accounting professional. She's a member of the National Association for Female Executives (NAFE).

Becky has served in various capacities in church ministry, including director of new members' orientation, liaison for the Full Gospel Baptist Church Fellowship and Sunday school teacher. In 1997, she founded The Christ*Land* Foundation. Its fundraising capital is earmarked for the construction of a retreat center and outreach ministry.

Appendix

Consumer Resource Guide

- **Business Inquiries**

  Better Business Bureau

  www.bbb.org/about/

  Provides reports on businesses that will be helpful

  before making a purchase of goods and/or services

- **Consumer Advocate**

  Clark Howard Talk Radio

  www.clarkhoward.com

  (877) 87-CLARK

  How to spend less, save more and avoid getting ripped off

- **Consumer Product Ratings**

  Consumer Reports

  www.consumerreports.org

  A good consumer buying guide

- **Debt Statistics**

  Federal Reserve Statistical Releases

  www.bog.frb.fed.us/releases/G19

  Get the latest facts about consumer credit

- **Credit Bureaus**
- **Equifax**

  www.equifax.com

  P.O. Box 105496

  Atlanta, GA 30348-5496

  (800) 997-2493

- **Experian (TRW)**

  www.experian.com

  505 City Parkway West

  Orange, CA 92868

  (888) 397-3742

- **Trans Union LLC**

  www.tuc.com

  P.O. Box 2000

  Chester, PA 19022

  (800) 888-4213

  (800) 916-8800

  Find out what they're saying about you

- **Debt Management & Consolidation**

  Consumer Credit Counseling Service

  (800) 251-CCCS

  Online Keywords: consumer credit counseling service -

  for your local area

  When your debt becomes overwhelming

- **Financial Advisor**

  Charles Ross, President

  Financial Media Services

  To schedule a seminar write or call:

  P.O. Box 870928

  Stone Mountain, GA 30087

  (404) 524-3830

  Workshops designed to teach biblical principals to

  managing your money

- **Home Financing Expert**

  www.realestate.com/buyersandsellers/lendingplus/

  financing_options.asp

  Get connected with a mortgage professional in your area

- **Investment and Financial Services**

  www.investinga-z.com

  Complete financial resource center

- **Money and Banking**

  Federal Reserve Board

  www.federalreserve.gov/

  Current information on the money and

  banking industry

PERSONAL BUDGET

INCOME:			Total
Gross Income			
Deductions:			
Other Income:			
Net Income			
EXPENSES:			
Tithes			
Save			
Mortgage / Rent			
Car Note			
Auto Insurance			
Automobile—fuel & cleaning			
Oil Change			
Clothes			
Lawn Care			
Electric (utility)			
Gas (utility)			
Telephone (utility)			
Water (utility)			
Garbage			
Cellular Phone			
Pager			
Cable TV			
Food			
Bank Service Charges			
Nails			
Hair			
Personal (toiletries, etc.)			
Entertainment—movies, dining, music			
Total Expenses			

UNSECURED DEBT
PAYMENT ALLOCATION

B	C	D		F
	__/__/__			__/__/__
ACCOUNT ACTIVITY	**Balance**	**Interest**	**Payment**	**Balance**

MONTHLY ACCOUNT ACTIVITY
AND
TIMELINE PROJECTION

A	B	C	D	E	F	G
1	**NAME OF ACCOUNTS**	Account Balances @ __/__/__	Annual Interest Rate	Monthly Interest Rate	Payment Allocation Percent	Monthly Payment Amount
2				+D2 / 12	+C2 / C12	+F2 * G12
3				+D3 / 12	+C3 / C12	+F3 * G12
4				+D4 / 12	+C4 / C12	+F4 * G12
5				+D5 / 12	+C5 / C12	+F5 * G12
6				+D6 / 12	+C6 / C12	+F6 * G12
7				+D7 / 12	+C7 / C12	+F7 * G12
8				+D8 / 12	+C8 / C12	+F8 * G12
9				+D9 / 12	+C9 / C12	+F9 * G12
10				+D10 / 12	+C10 / C12	+F10 * G12
11				+D11 / 12	+C11 / C12	+F11 * G12
12	Total				100%	$

UNSECURED DEBT
PAYMENT ALLOCATION

A	B	C	D	E	F	G
1	NAME OF ACCOUNTS	Account Balances @ _/_/_	Annual Interest Rate	Monthly Interest Rate	Payment Allocation Percent	Monthly Payment Amount
2				+D2 / 12	+C2 / C12	+F2 * G12
3				+D3 / 12	+C3 / C12	+F3 * G12
4				+D4 / 12	+C4 / C12	+F4 * G12
5				+D5 / 12	+C5 / C12	+F5 * G12
6				+D6 / 12	+C6 / C12	+F6 * G12
7				+D7 / 12	+C7 / C12	+F7 * G12
8				+D8 / 12	+C8 / C12	+F8 * G12
9				+D9 / 12	+C9 / C12	+F9 * G12
10				+D10 / 12	+C10 / C12	+F10 * G12
11				+D11 / 12	+C11 / C12	+F11 * G12
12	Total				100%	$

Spreadsheet Formulas
(Input cell G12 from Personal Budget)

MONTHLY ACCOUNT ACTIVITY
AND
TIMELINE PROJECTION

A	B	C	D	E	F
		_ /_ /_			_ /_ /_
1	NAME OF ACCOUNTS	Balance	Interest	Payment	Balance
2			+C2 * (I)		@SUM(C2+D2)-E2
3			+C3 * (I)		@SUM(C3+D3)-E3
4			+C4 * (I)		@SUM(C4+D4)-E4
5			+C5 * (I)		@SUM(C5+D5)-E5
6			+C6 * (I)		@SUM(C6+D6)-E6
7			+C7 * (I)		@SUM(C7+D7)-E7
8			+C8 * (I)		@SUM(C8+D8)-E8
9					
10					
11					
12	Total				

Spreadsheet Formulas

(I) = Interest rate taken from Column E of Unsecured Debt Payment
Allocation Spreadsheet

BIBLIOGRAPHY

Federal Reserve Board. *Consumer Credit*. U.S. Government, 1999

Richards, Chris J. *Consumer Debt Statistics*. Debt Control, Emerald Publishing, 1998

Cyber Nation. *13,000 Quotations to Inspire and Motivate You*. Nevada, 2000

Patterson, Ben. *Waiting*. InterVarsity Press, 1989

Consumer Credit Counseling Service. *Debt Repayment Plan*. Atlanta, GA, 2000

The Living Bible. Tyndale House Publishers. Wheaton, IL. 1981

INDEX

A

B

C

D

David,, 35-36
debt, xvii, xxi-7, 9, 11-12, 14-15, 17-20, 22-27, 29, 32, 37, 39-40, 43-44, 47, 55-56, 59-60, 65, 69-70, 77-78, 82-83, 86-89
    calculate,, 23, 27, 30, 44
    challenge of,, xxiii-xxiv
    control,, xvii, 10, 65, 68-69, 89
    evolution of,, xxi-xxiii
    repayment plan,, 4, 23, 43, 89
    solution to,, xxiv-xxv, 69
    unsecured,, xxiii, 23, 29, 32, 86-88
decisions, responsible, 12, 67

E

Elizabeth,, 36-37

F

facts and figures,, xxvii
faint factor,, 45
faith factor,, 47
focus factor,, 43
free, now that you are, 67-68
freedom, xxiii, 4, 7-8, 12, 14, 16, 25, 30, 40, 60, 65-67, 78
    financial,, xv, 1, 3, 7-12, 17, 19, 22, 26-27, 35, 53, 56-57, 60, 62-66, 69-70, 77-79, 83-84
    keys to,, 7
    visualize,, 14, 40
future, coming, 70-71

R

S

T

W

Contact information:

Becky McClain
c/o The ChristLand Foundation
P.O. Box 468686
Atlanta, GA 31146
christland@aol.com